T0346803

AROUND HOYLAND

HOYLAND

THEN & NOW

IN COLOUR

GEOFFREY HOWSE

This book is dedicated to the memory of Edward B. (Ted) Masheder and Joan Masheder

First published in 2012

The History Press
The Mill, Brimscombe Port
Stroud, Gloucestershire, GL5 2QG
www.thehistorypress.co.uk

British Library Cataloguing in Publication Data.
A catalogue record for this book is available from the British Library.

ISBN 978 0 7524 7005 4

Typesetting and origination by The History Press
Printed in India.

CONTENTS

ACKNOWLEDGEMENTS

Iris Ackroyd (1925-2012), Mary Ackroyd, Stuart Ackroyd, Victoria Ackroyd, Jessica Andrews, Keith Atack, Vera Atack, Keith Bamforth, Marlene Bamforth, Michael Barber, Susan Barber, Carole Baxter, Philip I. (Sam) Baxter, Caroline Bostwick, Daniel Bostwick, Fay Bostwick, Josh Bostwick, Laura Bostwick, Luke Bostwick, Neil Bostwick, Paul Bostwick, Sue Bostwick Tony Briggs, Liz Burgess, Robert Burgess, George W. Cooke, Kathleen Dale, Robert A. Dale, Iris Deller, Joanna C. Murray Deller, Ricky S. Deller, Tracy P. Deller, Christine Dulson, Gary Dulson, Angela Elliott, Brian Elliott, Percy Fellowes, Joyce Finney, Keith Froggatt, Les Gaddass, Margaret Gaddass, Brenda Gill, David Greenfield, Pamela Greenfield, Sandra Hague, George Hardy, Gary Hibberd, Karen Hibberd, Sheila Hibberd, Elaine Hickman, Steven Hickman, Keith Hopkinson, Ann Howse, Doreen Howse, Kathleen Howse, William (Bill) Hoyland, Raymond Mellor Jones, Alan Liptrot, Kristin Liptrot, Christine Johnson, Martyn Johnson, Diane Kelly, Edith Kelly, Frank Kelly, Peter Kelly, Mark Knights, Michael Lambert, Doug McHale, Yvonne McHale, Lynda Mallison, Julie Masheder, Kenneth Masheder, Stuart Masheder, Edwin Moody, Bob Mortimer, Graham Noble, Tom Noble, Vale Noble, Barbara Nelder, Eleanor Nelder, Stanley Nelder, Terry Nelder, Brian O'Shaughnessy, Sheila Margaret Ottley (1923-2012), Horace (Oscar) Platts 1925-2011, Kathleen Platts, Anthony Richards, David J. Richardson, Kathleen M. Robinson, Lindy Stevenson, Carl Swift, Michelle Tilling, Barry Turner, Percy Turner, Rose Vickers, Adam R. Walker, Anna Walker, Arthur O. Walker, Christine Walker, Darren J. Walker, Emma C. Walker, Ivan P. Walker, Jenny Walker, Paula L. Walker, Suki B. Walker, Thomas A. Walker, Walker's Newsagents (Hoyland), Lanza Watson, Clifford Willoughby, Margaret Willoughby, Betty Young, Roy Young. I would also like to thank John D. Murray, who has assisted me over many years; and finally, not forgetting my ever-faithful walking companion, Coco.

ABOUT THE AUTHOR

Geoffrey Howse, actor, author and historian, was born in Sheffield and grew up in Elsecar and Hoyland. He is an avid writer of local history books and has become well-known for his writing and books about Yorkshire subjects, including his three *Around Hoyland* titles in the Britain in Old Photographs series. His recent titles include *A Century of Sheffield*, *Sheffield Then & Now*, *Doncaster Then & Now* and *The Little Book of Yorkshire*, all published by The History Press.

INTRODUCTION

Situated within the West Riding of Yorkshire, within that portion which has for generations been referred to as South Yorkshire, is a unique region at the heart of which lies Hoyland Nether, which today covers an area totalling 1,999 acres, and consists of the township of Hoyland, Hoyland Common, Platts Common and Milton, the hamlets of Upper Hoyland and Skiers Hall and the village of Elsecar, which incorporates the areas known as St Helens, Cobcar and Stubbin.

The area around Hoyland is very special indeed. Its uniqueness lies in its development over 1,000 years. It is a microcosm of agricultural, architectural and industrial development, whose historical significance is without equal. The area has all the necessary component parts of this model of rural and urban, agricultural and industrial development, on a scale and with a quality which can be found nowhere else in England.

Sadly, many local residents remain blissfully unaware of the tremendous heritage to be found in their immediate surroundings, their understanding being exacerbated by the enormous void left by the loss of many industries, in addition to the huge amount of destruction of fine properties that has taken place mostly within Hoyland itself in comparatively recent years. Notwithstanding the major losses of many of its finest buildings, the township has continued to suffer in one way or another, notably from unsympathetic building projects.

In selecting the old images I have attempted to highlight some of the major changes that have taken place. I have neglected to include some very fine and famous subjects featured in my previous *Around Hoyland* books, such as Tankersley Old Hall, Wentworth Woodhouse and Wentworth Castle. The changes at these locations have been minimal and their inclusion here would not be appropriate.

As Hoyland's fortunes increase during the renaissance it is undergoing, it is hoped that several of its sleeping beauties, dormant for many years, will be restored and brought back to life, revitalising and refreshing the entire area. Despite the odd, but perhaps inevitable, drawbacks which are likely to be encountered on the way to greater prosperity, Hoyland's future is looking brighter than it has for decades.

Geoffrey Howse, 2012

HOYLAND TOWN HALL

HOYLAND TOWN HALL, High Street, seen from Market Street in around 1903, was originally built as a Mechanics' Institute in 1840. In 1891 a local board was formed to run the affairs of the growing community. Its headquarters were in the Town Hall. The local board was replaced three years later when Hoyland Urban District Council was formed, under the terms of the 1894 Local Government Act. The stones of the clock tower, added in 1892 to provide another amenity thanks to the benevolence of local businesswoman Martha Knowles, are mellowing and acquiring the sooty coating characteristic of the rest of the structure. Over the years that followed, the clock became affectionately known as 'Old Martha'. The newly positioned horse trough was erected to celebrate the reign of Queen Victoria and the coronation of King Edward Vll.
(Doreen Howse Collection)

THE PRESENT-DAY Town Hall, largely built of extremely expensive hand-made bricks, to an unimaginative, mundane design, houses the Co-operative supermarket on the ground floor. This building was constructed around the old Town Hall and opened in June 1973, with its entrance front facing the newly created Southgate, the Town Hall staff simply having decanted from the old building to the new, at which point demolition of the old building began. The large windows to the left on the second floor show the position of the Council Chamber. Hoyland UDC survived until the unwarranted and unwanted major local government changes of 1974, since when the Town Hall has served as offices for Barnsley MBC, as well as, at one juncture, a Job Centre. If plans are implemented for the second phase of the town centre redevelopment, the Town Hall will be completely demolished within the next two or three years, or possibly even earlier.

HIGH STREET, HOYLAND

THIS EARLY EDWARDIAN view shows High Street, looking towards Post Office Buildings at the junction of Milton Road and West Street. E. James's draper and hatter's shop can be seen in the background, at No. 1 Milton Road. Next door, to the right of James's premises, situated at No. 2 West Street, is Fred Ford's stationary shop. The first building on the left of the photograph is one of Hoyland's licensed beerhouses (no wines and spirits on sale), the Gardeners Arms, which was kept by George Smith during this period. His name can just be discerned on the sign immediately above the advertisement for Wheatley's Hop Bitters. In the right foreground is the front garden wall of Holly House.
(Chris Sharp of Old Barnsley)

HIGH STREET IN the autumn of 2011. On the left, at the junction of High Croft – on a site which until only a few months previously had been occupied by the replacement for the original Gardeners Arms and the building built for the supermarket chain Kwik Save, and latterly occupied by the much missed

Factory Outlet Store – is the recently opened library. This excellent facility replaced Hoyland's former library, which was situated (until its recent demolition, now occupied by much-needed parking facilities) in a prefabricated concrete-and-wood clad structure at the other end of High Croft, opposite the Bethany Mission. That library was itself a replacement for the township's first library, which once occupied part of the Miners' Welfare building in King Street. It originally served as the Labour Exchange. Escaping the trend of many other areas throughout England where library closures are rife, Hoyland is indeed fortunate. The library forms part of The Hoyland Centre. On the right is Tina's Deli & Café, and beyond is Little M's Fish and Chip Shop with its upstairs restaurant. Next door, at No. 8 High Street, is Guest's butchers shop. In the middle distance, across the recently constructed car park occupying the site of Post Office Buildings, demolished over three decades previously, can be seen Hoyland Town Belmont Working Men's Club.

HIGH STREET, HOYLAND

HIGH STREET, HOYLAND, *c.*1920. The John Knowles Memorial church was built in the gap between Holly House and Herbert Garner's ironmongers. The church was erected after the new vicar of St Peter's, the Revd Charles William Bennett, placed a brass cross and two candlesticks on the altar. These items were a gift from the parishioners of the church he had recently served as curate. The parishioners of the then chapel of ease, St Andrew's, were outraged at what they considered to be his Papist leanings. One of them, Mrs Elizabeth Bartlett, the only daughter of Martha Knowles (benefactress of the Town Hall clock), was so incensed that she erected, at her own expense, a new church for the Free Church of England, and named it in memory of her brother, who had died, at the age of fifty-two, in 1899.

The foundation stones were laid on 20 September 1911. All the buildings seen in this view remain today, including Holly House, which might be a surprise to some. To the right of the church can be

seen Herbert Garner's ironmongers; next door is Wilkinson's tobacconists and sweet shop and beyond, at the corner of Market Street, is Bellamy's Boot Stores. (*Frank Kelly Collection*)

IN 1927 HOLLY HOUSE was purchased from the Firth family (the well-known elocution and drama teacher Miss Florence D. Firth lived at Holly House as a child, until it was sold) by Mr and Mrs Harry Cooper. Two double-fronted shops were built, covering the garden where the holly bush from which Holly House took its name once grew. Mrs Cooper and her sister Mrs Storey had been running a drapery business in a small shop in King Street since just after the First World War. They moved into the two-storey shop next to the church and traded as Storey & Cooper. The other shop built onto the front of Holly House was rented to Melias, a grocery firm. Today, Melias' premises are occupied by the fashion boutique Utopia, and Storey & Cooper's former premises are split between Hall's fruit, vegetable and flower shop (members of the Hall family have occupied various shops in the area for over a century) and Hoyland Pets & Garden Centre, run by Karen Hibberd. Flats occupy the upper storey of the entire building; these spaces once formed part of the retail premises. If one follows the line of the wall adjacent to John Knowles Memorial church, the stone gable of Holly House can be clearly seen attached to the red bricks of the extension. Beyond Walker's Newsagents at No. 2 Market Street is the National Westminster Bank, and across the road, at No. 2 King Street, the off-licence Rhythm & Booze, one of a chain.

HIGH STREET
AND
MILTON ROAD,
HOYLAND

HIGH STREET VIEWED from the junction of Milton Road with West Street, photographed by Ted Masheder, 1960. On the left, Guest's butchers, Higgs's fish and chip shop, Higgs's off-licence, and set back, the gable above Melias's shop, then Storey & Cooper can be seen. Beyond John Knowles Memorial church, with the blind extended, is Walker's Newsagents, and behind the Thames Trader lorry belonging to the Don Bakery of Sheffield can be seen Roland Cross & Son's premises. *(Masheder Family Collection)*

HIGH STREET, SEEN in the late summer of 2011. The premises of Guest's, a noted Hoyland butcher for five generations spanning 130 years, has recently been put up

for sale. However, in March 2012 the shop's owner, sixty-four-year-old Chris Guest, decided to put off his retirement and took down the 'for sale' notice. Chris started helping out at the age of nine before taking charge at twenty-two when his father died. Chris said: 'Boys in the family take over the business but I've got three girls so I've no-one to pass it on to. We're the only traditional butchers left in Hoyland and we're at the mercy of the supermarkets and the overpriced farm shops.' He received a number of offers for the premises but only two from people who intended to retain its current use and they were put off because of the plans to build a Tesco superstore in the town.

On the right is a newly constructed building known as the Hoyland Centre, incorporating a GP surgery, Hoyland Library & Connects Centre, Children, Young People & Family Centre, café and the Co-operative Pharmacy, which occupies the blue coloured part of the building in the right foreground.

NORTH SIDE OF HIGH STREET, HOYLAND

ISAAC LICHMERE WALKER (1885-1958) set up in business in Hoyland after working with his father at his newsagent's business in Graham's Orchard, Barnsley, in the 1880s. Lichie Walker, as he became known, settled in Hoyland and began to trade as a confectioner. Then, in the early 1920s, he took over the newsagent's business that his aunt, Mrs Rothwell, had purchased from John Thompson, at No. 8 King Street, where he continued to make confectionary at the back of his shop. On 17 May 1932 Herbert Garner, the ironmonger, died suddenly. Lichie saw an opportunity to expand into larger premises, so he took over Garner's shop and moved from his King Street premises to No. 22 High Street, where his sign can be seen above the large bay window

which had been a prominent feature of Garner's old shop. Taken in around 1935, this photograph also shows the recently opened draper's Storey & Cooper, and next door is Melias's. The grocers and tea dealers Melias was founded by Daniel Melia of Manchester, in 1896. Originally trading as Daniel Melia & Co. Ltd, from the 1920s to the 1960s they traded as Melias's Ltd, with branches in various parts of the country. Beyond Melias' can be seen Chambers' sweet shop. In the foreground, at No. 2 Market Street, is the National Provincial Bank.
(Walker's Newsagents Collection)

ALL THE BUILDINGS seen in the 1930s view, with the exception of Post Office Buildings, seen on the extreme left, remain. This section of High Street is virtually the only part of Hoyland town centre that escaped the wholesale obliteration of most of the township's better commercial buildings during the early 1970s.

HIGH STREET AND POST OFFICE BUILDINGS, HOYLAND

HIGH STREET IN the early 1960s. On the left is No. 13, which was at that time occupied by the Labour Exchange, having formerly been Beatties Busy Corner and before that Moses Fletcher's Old Eccles Cake Shop. The distinctive John Smith's Brewery inn sign can be seen beyond the Rover 3 litre parked on the left. The sign is on the forecourt of the Gardeners Arms, which had replaced the original public house bearing the same name, the forecourt of the newer building occupying the site of the original public house. In the distance are Post Office Buildings; Alfred Ellaway's newsagents at No. 1 Milton Road can be seen on the left of May Taylor's ladies and childrens outfitters, No. 2 West Street. The gable end displaying the Oakwell Ales sign belongs to Higg's off-licence, grocery and sweet shop. Outside Walker's Newsagents, with its newly installed shop front, can be seen another model of the Rover marque, a

Rover 90. Next door to Walker's at No. 24, in the immediate right foreground, is Claude Ellestone's tobacconists and sweet shop. When Douglas Porteous Beattie, of Beattie's Busy Corner, retired just before the Second World War, Lichie Walker took over his bus and railway agencies. He was eventually joined in the business by his son, Geoff (1914-95), whose own son, David, later joined him. In 1971, Walker's took over Maurice Layte's newsagents in King Street after his retirement and incorporated it into their own. In 1974 they took over Claude Ellestone's shop next door at No. 24, using it as gardening shop and card shop, until it was incorporated into their own premises in 1997 and a new shop front installed across Nos 22-24, with a re-positioned double entrance door. *(Walker's Newsagents Collection)*

IN FEBRUARY 2005 Walker's took over Thawley's newsagents, situated in Ottley's old shop in King Street. Walker's continued to trade there, under the name Thawley's, until June 2010, when the business was transferred to their main shop and their King Street premises rented to Priceless Discount Store. Today, Walkers is run by David Walker, his wife Christine, their daughter Suki and six staff. This present-day view looks across High Street and down High Croft.

The Town Hall, on the left, occupies the site of Beattie's Busy Corner, and on the right-hand side Hoyland's new library can be seen, which forms part of the recently opened complex of facilities housed in a curiously fashioned structure in an mixture of diverse architectural styles. The entrance to the complex is up the ramp seen on the right in High Croft. The roof of the Bethany Mission can be seen in the centre background, across Southgate.

KING STREET AND HIGH STREET, HOYLAND

KING STREET AND High Street, Hoyland, in the mid-1960s. In the left foreground, standing empty, is the Turf Tavern (owned by Samuel Smith's Tadcaster Brewery, and licensed as a beerhouse only). It closed in 1960. Next door, set back and out of sight, is Maurice Layte's newsagents. Next to that is Clayton's furniture shop. The steps leading to Tal Lowbridge's barber's shop project onto the pavement (part of his barber's pole can be seen), and a lady is looking into the window of the Globe Tea Co., situated at the corner of George Street at No. 1 King Street. In the right foreground, Ottley's former premises are tenanted by Woodhouse's, a grocers with a butchery department. Lichie Walker's old shop at No. 8 King Street is occupied by Don Valley Cleaners Ltd, and at No. 6, with its incongruous slatted wood 1960s shop front, is E. Norwood's opticians. The canopy of Maltby's

the greengrocers can be seen over their shop, the lintel over the door of which has the inscription G. B. 1804, indicating the Georgian origins of these particular buildings. The gable of the premises of Roland Cross & Son can be seen above the roof of Maltby's premises.
(Walker's Newsagents Collection)

THE CONTEMPORARY VIEW of King Street and High Street clearly shows the tragic losses Hoyland's architecture has suffered since the early 1970s. In King Street only Ottley's old shop in the right foreground remains intact and is currently rented from Walker's by Priceless Discount Store, part of a small chain of discount shops, which have a distinctive though somewhat garish livery of mauve and lime green. In the left foreground is Barclays Bank, with Premier Eyecare opticians next door. Occupying the first floor of these buildings is the Karen Murillo School of Dance, with Jack Fulton (frozen food and other supplies) beyond and bookmakers Ladbrokes at No. 1 King Street. Market Street and High Street can be seen in the centre background.

KING STREET, HOYLAND

KING STREET, HOYLAND, *c.*1905. On the left, grocer Roland Cross & Son is trading from the premises previously owned by Wards, who had taken over from the Knowles family towards the end of the nineteenth century. The shop stands at the corner of King Street and Market Street, with a window placed each side of its recessed doorway. The interior was low ceilinged and dark. Displayed in the left window was a range of dry goods, such as prunes, currants, butter beans, split peas, lentils and pearl barley. On the right were such items as bacon, ham and cheese. On the right can be seen the barber's pole outside William Thomas Lowbridge's shop, his engraved glass window proclaiming his premises a 'hair cutting and shaving saloon'. His son, Harold Oxspring (Tal) Lowbridge, would shortly succeed his father in the business. John Thompson's furniture shop is next door to Lowbridge's,

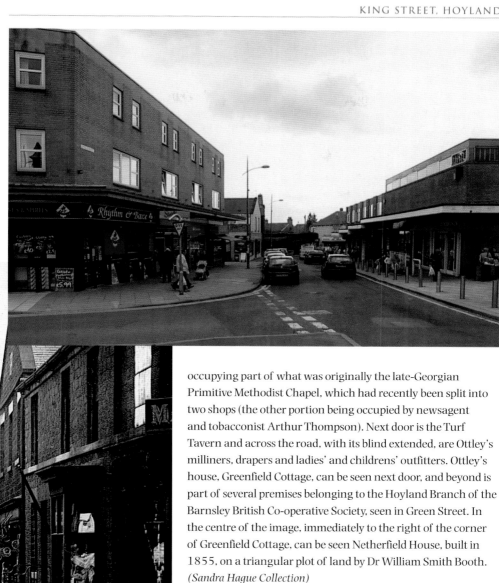

occupying part of what was originally the late-Georgian Primitive Methodist Chapel, which had recently been split into two shops (the other portion being occupied by newsagent and tobacconist Arthur Thompson). Next door is the Turf Tavern and across the road, with its blind extended, are Ottley's milliners, drapers and ladies' and childrens' outfitters. Ottley's house, Greenfield Cottage, can be seen next door, and beyond is part of several premises belonging to the Hoyland Branch of the Barnsley British Co-operative Society, seen in Green Street. In the centre of the image, immediately to the right of the corner of Greenfield Cottage, can be seen Netherfield House, built in 1855, on a triangular plot of land by Dr William Smith Booth. *(Sandra Hague Collection)*

THE LOSS TO Hoyland's townscape and future generations which occurred from the 1950s well into the 1970s (when some of the area's finest buildings were consigned to rubble) is almost incalculable. Hoyland should be at the hub of this historically important and rapidly expanding centre for tourism. Instead, because its finer features have largely been obliterated, Hoyland itself sticks out from most of its neighbours like the proverbial sore thumb, and sadly, today very little of what remains, particularly in the town centre itself, merits a second glance.

21

KING STREET, HOYLAND

KING STREET, HOYLAND, seen from the gate of Greenfield Cottage, *c.*1900. In the left foreground is the Co-op drapery store, which also housed a milliners and ladies' clothing department on the first floor. Beyond the properties on the right, at the corner of Hall Street, is William Joll's glass and china shop. Opposite Joll's can be seen the sign of J.E. Matthews's chemist shop, at No. 26 King Street. Further down the street on the right is the Co-op grocery store, and in the distance are the single-storey shops situated below the Mount Tabor Primitive Methodist Chapel.
(Sandra Hague Collection)

TODAY, THE BUILDINGS that survive in this part of King Street serve as a sad reminder to many of Hoyland's once considerably more diverse shopping facilities. Occupying the two storeys of the former Co-op Drapery store is Hoyland Discount Furniture. Next door, in what was once the Co-op butcher's, is a shop run by Barnsley Animal Rescue Charity. On the extreme right, occupying No. 2 Hall Street, is Magnolia Hair & Beauty. There are three empty shops and no fewer than four take-away food outlets, where once many of Hoyland's finest purveyors of comestibles plied their trades. In my youth, which was not so long ago, I can remember there being five butchers' shops in King Street alone; today there are none. I can recall no fewer than fourteen such shops in the immediate area (although I'm told there were once many more). Jump butcher Percy Turner told me that in Hoyland Common alone there were once seven butcher's shops; now only Butterworth's survives. Presently there are only three butcher's shops in the entire area. Similarly, of the thirty-one corner shops I can remember during the 1960s and '70s in Hoyland Common, Hoyland, Milton, Platts Common and Elsecar, sadly only two have survived.

23

KING STREET, HOYLAND

A LATE 1950s view of King Street taken by Arthur Roberts. On the left beyond the Vanity Box (ladies' hairdressers) is the opening into Bethel Street, on the other corner of which stands what was once the Five Alls public house. This establishment closed in 1939, and survived as a private residence until its demolition in 1973. Above its pitched roof can just be glimpsed the corner of the impressively pedimented façade of Bethel Chapel, which is made of Portland Stone. The chapel's foundation stone was laid on 25 October 1880. On the right are a group of single-storey shops and office premises, beyond which is the gable of the building partly occupied by Reg and Elsie Dewhirst's confectionary, tobacco and provisions shop, which had a distinctive, bright-yellow painted shop front. In the right foreground a narrow unmetalled road runs along the side of Mount Tabor Primitive Methodist Chapel (commonly known as the 'Prims'), which graced Hoyland's townscape from 1880 until 1963. *(Reproduced with kind permission of Lynda Mallison)*

IN THE PRESENT day the road configuration has altered. Southgate goes off to the right, where the Prims once stood, and terminates at the junction with Milton Road. On the left, beyond the Vanity Box, is the renamed Bethel Street, know known as Fitzwilliam Close, where a delightful small shop known as Bits & Bobs is situated behind the hairdressing salon, selling a selection of fancy goods in addition to curios and second hand items. Across the road, the recently opened Fitzwilliam Court offers high-quality sheltered independent accommodation for older people and is one of the better structures to have been built locally in recent years. It covers the site of the Five Alls, Bethel Chapel and various houses, shops and cottages which once formed part of King Street, Bethel Street and Victoria Street. Most of the properties on the right of the 1950s image were demolished over four decades ago. Their site is one of many such sadly neglected and ill-used eyesores pock-marking the Hoyland area.

GEORGE STREET, HOYLAND, VIEWED FROM HIGH CROFT

HOYLAND MARKET, LAID out at the back of the Town Hall on its temporary site, in October 1970. Hoyland police station (built in 1889) can be seen in George Street (second building from the right). Encouraged by Hoyland Nether UDC, a London-based firm, the Grasim Group of Companies re-opened Hoyland Market on 24 October 1970. I can remember it distinctly, as it was on my birthday. Barnsley Council tried to invoke a charter forbidding anyone from opening a market within a 7-mile radius of Barnsley, but they were on to a non-starter as the precedent had already been made by Hoyland's former

market. Within less than two years the market had been moved back to the site of the original incarnation, opening on 10 June 1972, under the control of Hoyland UDC.
(Masheder Family Collection)

WITHIN TWO YEARS of the older image, all of the buildings featured had been demolished. Hoyland police station was demolished in 1972 and a new police station opened in Hoyland Road, Hoyland Common. From that day to the present time the frequency of policing locally has diminished considerably. Once a virtually permanent presence, the appearance of a member of the police force in Hoyland town centre today more often than not gives rise to tongue-in-cheek comments concerning the rarity of the breed. The upper part of George Street, prominent in the 1970s view, has completely disappeared. A car park now occupies the site and the buildings seen in the background, revealed by the demolition of the police station and other buildings, are in Hall Street.

WEST STREET, HOYLAND

A VIEW OF the corner of Post Office Buildings and West Street from the junction with Milton Road and High Street, captured by Ted Masheder in 1970. Amongst the shops on the left can be seen the corner of Jessie Matsell's ladies' outfitters, Ben Sorby's fishmonger's and Jack Hall's fruit and vegetable shop. On the right, the former gas showrooms, once Mell's joiners and undertakers, is occupied by Taylor's electrical shop, above which Gallon's stores' former premises are standing empty. Gallon's were one of three new 'chain' grocery stores which opened in Hoyland between the wars, the others being Brough's and Melias's. Brough's was a very large store which opened further up West Street, on the left-hand side; the building is now occupied by Allendale Building Supplies, whose roof can be seen on the left skyline behind the twin end gables of Fieldhead House. Melias was situated in High Street.

The entrance to Naylor's Yard can be seen beyond the lamp post on the left, and Belmont Yard goes off to the left at the other side of the building with the first-floor bay windows – which once housed Hoyland's Liberal Club – before the double-fronted stuccoed detached cottage. West Street was originally known as Finkle Street and both in and around the area seen here was where many nail makers once had their homes and workshops during the seventeenth, eighteenth and nineteenth centuries, possibly even earlier. Many nail makers also worked in farming, mostly during the summer months, nail working being reserved for the months of poorer weather.
(Masheder Family Collection)

POST OFFICE BUILDINGS were demolished in 1981 and Gallon's former store disappeared around the same period. Taylor's former electrical shop was latterly occupied by D. & P. Hirst but the premises have stood empty for several years. At the time of writing some refurbishment work has been taking place.

PRINCESS THEATRE, WEST STREET, HOYLAND

A LATE EDWARDIAN view of West Street. The Princess Theatre, whose enormous gabled façade fronts West Street, was built by the Hoyland firm John Parr and Sons and opened on Boxing Day 1893, with Lawrence Daly's company in a performance of *Cissie*. The auditorium was well appointed, with a private box on each side of the stage. The balcony, pit stalls, pit and gallery held 150, 200, 360 and 300 people respectively. There was also standing room available. On the opening night, the theatre was packed and hundreds were turned away. The Princess Theatre specialised in melodrama, a popular form of entertainment at that time, and many professional touring theatre companies played there. Its first owner was William Ottley, who until his death in 1914 was the proprietor of the drapery and millinery shop in King Street. After his death it continued under the care of his widow. In addition to 'legitimate' theatre productions such as *The Corsican Brothers* and *The Sign of the Cross* were staged there. A comedian from one of these shows married the widowed landlady of the Queen's Head. Local amateurs also appeared there;

one of them, Roy Colville, was a photographer. He played many leading roles in the productions staged at the theatre. Prices ranged from 15s for a box or 3s 6d for a single seat; a seat in the balcony cost 2s. For a seat in the pit stalls the price was 1s 6d; the pit cost 9d, and the gallery 6d. By 1902 silent films were often shown between the acts of plays, and by the 1920s live shows were no longer a feature. The Princess's interior was altered to increase the size of the auditorium and eventually adapted to become a fully-fledged picture palace, with a projection suite built onto the front gable.
(Sandra Hague Collection)

IN THE BOOK *Curtains!!! Or A New Life for Old Theatres*, Christopher Brereton lists the theatre as the Empire Hippodrome (formerly the Princess Theatre). However, for most of its life since the 1920s the theatre has been known by the Americanised German name 'Kino'. The Kino has not shown films for decades, the last film being screened there on 5 May 1962. It became a bingo hall, and then served for a brief period as a snooker hall. Quite recently, this once grand theatre became used as a function suite and for salsa and fitness dance classes. Like so many fine amenities that once existed in and around Hoyland, far too many of which have disappeared forever, one wonders if local people appreciate and are truly aware of the potential significance of this important survival. The tower of the Italianate St Helen's Roman Catholic church (opened in 1929) can be seen in the centre background.

MARKET STREET, HOYLAND

A VIEW OF Market Street taken from the junction of King Street and High Street, c.1900. Bellamy's Boot Stores and Colville's grocers and tobacconists can be seen in the left foreground. The tall, fortress-like building is the Wesleyan Chapel of 1809. Methodism was introduced into Hoyland by John Johnson of Barley Hall, Thorpe Hesley. Mr Johnson came to live at Manor Farm in about 1747, after which Methodist preachers often stayed there. John Wesley preached from the Tithe Lane steps in 1772. Interest in Methodism grew and in 1809 the chapel seen here was constructed at a cost of £800, on land donated by William Gray, the then occupant of Manor House Farm.

Beyond the Wesleyan Chapel, in premises facing the market at No. 14 Market Street, George Howarth is trading as a bespoke tailor, cycling tailor, ready-made clothier, hatter, hosier and general outfitter. Frank Smith & Co. were trading at No. 7 Market Street and advertised special lines in draperies and dress materials 'offered at the lowest possible prices for best quality'. *(Chris Thawley Collection)*

FROM 1932 HOYLAND'S Wesleyan Chapel became known as St Paul's, when the various Methodist sects in Hoyland amalgamated. The last service at St Paul's was held in May 1975, after which the congregation moved to the newly converted Thistle House, fronting Market Street and situated about 100 yards further along on the left between Duke Street and Tithe Laithe. This building was the former home and surgery of Dr Barclay Wiggins (1867-1959). St Paul's became Charisma Antiques, run by John Simmonds. It traded for over two decades until he retired, and the building was then sold and converted into a public house and nightclub, also called Charisma, arranged over three floors. The layout has been changed several times in recent years and at the time of writing the ground floor is being converted into retail facilities.

THE STRAFFORD ARMS AND HOYLAND CINEMA HOUSE

THE STRAFFORD ARMS and Hoyland Cinema House, early 1920s. Originally part of Earl Fitzwilliam's extensive estates, the Strafford Arms was known as The Beggar and Gentleman in the early nineteenth century. However, that name was short-lived, and it was decided to name it after Lord Fitzwilliam's ancestor Thomas Wentworth, 1st Earl of Strafford (1593-1641), known as 'the Great Earl of Strafford', who lived nearby at Wentworth Woodhouse.

Hoyland Cinema House was built in 1920, on a site previously occupied by Hoyland Market, by a group of local businessmen who formed the Hoyland Cinema Co., which gave Hoyland its much-needed third screen – such was the popularity of 'going to the pictures' during this period. The new cinema was sandwiched between the reduced market site and the Strafford Arms. It had stalls, balcony and seats upholstered in Prussian blue plush. The iron posts seen in the foreground date from the time when the original market opened in 1867: they were positioned there to mark the boundary of the market.
(Joan Hopson Collection)

IN THE PRESENT day, the same location is much changed. Hoyland Cinema House was Hoyland's last cinema to open and the first to close; it screened its final film in 1957. The building stood empty until it was demolished in November 1971. Its site is once again occupied by Hoyland Market. In the late 1970s what had become Hoyland's finest public house, the Strafford Arms, was irredeemably altered. All the rooms, including a very useful Concert Room (which had previously provided refuge for different groups of locals including the Hoyland Silver Prize Band, who practiced there), were knocked into one. In the 1980s the name was changed to The Beggar and The Gentleman but a few years later the additional 'the' was dropped and it became known by its original name, The Beggar and Gentleman. Even more recently, its name was simplified to 'Beggar and Gentleman', but to others this house is more commonly known as t' Beggar. Many local people still refer to this once fine hostelry as the 'Strafford'; others remain stunned that one of our greatest English statesmen, who had strong attachments to Hoyland, is no longer commemorated.

MARKET STREET

MARKET STREET,
c. 1905. On the right,
the large, double-fronted
house on the corner
of Spring Gardens is
Brentwood, No. 46.
This house was built for
Herbert Garner in the
late Edwardian period.
Herbert Garner owned
the ironmonger's shop at
No. 22 High Street. After
Garner's premature death
in 1932, Lichie Walker
took over his business
premises, and since then
Garner's former shop
has traded as Walker's
Newsagents.

HERBERT GARNER'S FORMER home is currently occupied by the Weedon family. Occupying the first house on the left, at No. 49, is Hoyland Family Dental Centre. Further down the terrace, at No. 35, in premises occupied for most of the last century by Thompson's second hand shop, is Homework, a shop selling a wide range of ironmongery, electrical, DIY, gardening and general household goods, which is popularly known locally as 'Little Woolworths'. Across the road at No. 40 is Blush, a shop offering made-to-order clothing and cosmetics, plus handbags and jewellery. At No. 38 is Escape hairdressing and beauty salon.

HOYLAND HALL

HOYLAND HALL, SEEN here in the Edwardian period, is arguably the finest Georgian building to have been built in Hoyland, and for almost 200 years was the town's principal residence. Records for whom and exactly when Hoyland Hall was built and the name of its architect have been lost. It may have been built on the site of an earlier hall, which is mentioned in documents dating back to 1579. However, it seems likely that some of these references actually refer to Upper Hoyland Hall, situated about half a mile away. Henry Hartop, a partner in the Milton Ironworks, who later ran Elsecar Ironworks for the 4th and 5th Earls Fitzwilliam, was resident here from the early 1820s until 1841, as was William Vizard, the first owner of Hoyland Silkstone Colliery. William Vizard (1774-1859) was the same William Vizard who acted as attorney to Queen Caroline during her trial in 1820.

His son, also called William, inherited the estate but did not long survive his father. He died in 1865 and the estate passed to his brother, the Revd Henry Brougham Vizard (1825-74), whose son, Harry William Vizard of Portland Place, Lyme Regis, Dorset, its last Vizard owner, put the estate up for sale in 1884. Hoyland

Hall subsequently served as a residence for various managers of Hoyland Silkstone Colliery until its closure in 1928, after which the managers of Rockingham Colliery lived there.
(Sandra Hague Collection)

AFTER HOYLAND HALL ceased to be a private residence, it was used for educational purposes for over twenty years. Some of its park was used to build a replacement for the Victorian Market Street School, once situated across the road from the hall. During the 1980s Hoyland Hall was boarded up and remained empty for several years. It was broken into by thieves and stripped of some of its chimney pieces and fittings. Towards the end of the decade, the hall was purchased by David Pearson to create a residential home for the elderly. The old hall was engulfed by extensions, making it the nucleus of a considerably larger building. Fortunately, these extensions were built in an architectural style which complements the original Georgian hall. Hoyland Hall Residential Home was officially opened by Her Royal Highness the Duchess of Kent on 6 June 1991.

MILTON ROAD, HOYLAND

EDWARD B. MASHEDER moved from Tankersley Lane to run Milton Motor Co. in 1948. This garage stood at the top of Milton Road, facing Hoyland's oldest licensed premises, the Ball Inn. The original garage and vehicle repair shop occupied the buildings to the right of

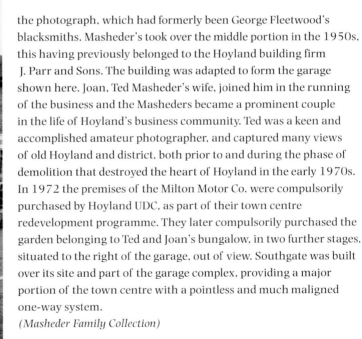

the photograph, which had formerly been George Fleetwood's blacksmiths. Masheder's took over the middle portion in the 1950s, this having previously belonged to the Hoyland building firm J. Parr and Sons. The building was adapted to form the garage shown here. Joan, Ted Masheder's wife, joined him in the running of the business and the Masheders became a prominent couple in the life of Hoyland's business community. Ted was a keen and accomplished amateur photographer, and captured many views of old Hoyland and district, both prior to and during the phase of demolition that destroyed the heart of Hoyland in the early 1970s. In 1972 the premises of the Milton Motor Co. were compulsorily purchased by Hoyland UDC, as part of their town centre redevelopment programme. They later compulsorily purchased the garden belonging to Ted and Joan's bungalow, in two further stages, situated to the right of the garage, out of view. Southgate was built over its site and part of the garage complex, providing a major portion of the town centre with a pointless and much maligned one-way system.

(Masheder Family Collection)

THE SITE OF Milton Motor Co. is today occupied by part of the recently opened complex of buildings known as The Hoyland Centre.

SHEFFIELD ROAD, HOYLAND COMMON

A 1920s VIEW of Sheffield Road, Hoyland Common, looking towards the crossroads with Hoyland Road and Tankersley Lane. The junction on the left at Hoyland Road was known as Allott's Corner, after the high-class bakers, confectioners and grocers whose shop occupied the corner site. The bakery was next door, in Hoyland Road, and in Sheffield Road, next to Allott's grocery, was Hemingway's hardware shop and Debarr's shoe shop. A Leyland Tiger omnibus on its way from Chapeltown is captured travelling towards Birdwell and on to Barnsley. Hoyland Common did not

exist as a village until after the Hoyland Enclosure Acts of the 1790s. During the eighteenth and early nineteenth centuries, some single-storey dwellings had been built to house miners and nailers. Nail making had been taking place in nearby Elsecar since the early seventeenth century and was also a feature of Hoyland's Finkle Street (renamed West Street), but by the end of the eighteenth century this cottage industry had become established in Hoyland Common, providing nails for the London market. Hoyland Common continued to grow throughout the nineteenth century, following the exploitation of the mineral resources, namely iron ore and coal, widely available locally; and all the buildings seen here were erected during that century.
(*Chris Sharp of Old Barnsley*)

ALTHOUGH ALLOTT'S HAVE not been trading in Hoyland Common for over forty years, people still ask for Allott's Corner when travelling by bus and alighting at the nearby stops in Sheffield Road and Hoyland Road. Hemingway's former premises is occupied by the Barber Shop Co. and Allott's corner site by their ladies' division, B Special Ladies Salon.

HOYLAND LAW SCHOOL

HOYLAND LAW SCHOOL, *c*.1895 (right). The turret of the Law Stand can be seen to the right of the school building, behind the tree. This school was one of many such establishments which educated Hoyland's children. Hoyland Law School (1838-1934) opened immediately after the closure of a school (which stood at the junction of Market Street with Mell Avenue), with George Armitage as its schoolmaster. In 1842 the school's pupils consisted of seventy-five boys and twenty-three girls. In 1850, the 5th Earl Fitzwilliam donated £25 10*s* for building work at the school, and a further £51 7*s* in 1851. In 1862 a new classroom was added, paid for by a National Society grant and monies from the trustees of George Ellis of Brampton.

Like his father before him, the 6th Earl Fitzwilliam continued to support the school, at the time known as Hoyland Law National School, and helped with building costs in 1866 with a donation of £27 10*s* for masons' work at the school and schoolhouse. In 1872 his Lordship also paid £10 8*s* for a new water pump. Hoyland Law

School continued to educate Hoyland's children, but after being placed on a blacklist by the Board of Education in 1925, it continued on a downward spiral. In 1933 its older pupils went to the nearby newly opened Kirk Balk School after the summer holidays. The younger children attended for a further year, until, in 1934, the school closed. The building was used for a time by St Peter's church as a Sunday school. After it fell into disrepair, the building was demolished in December 1939. *(Sandra Hague Collection)*

THE BUNGALOW THAT stands on part of the site once occupied by Hoyland Law School. In the front garden can be seen the foundations of the old school along with the stubs of the distinctive corner towers.

HOYLAND STAND

HOYLAND LAW STAND, seen here 6 May 1935, while it was being used as a private residence. Local residents pose by the bonfire built to mark Hoyland's final event of the Silver Jubilee celebrations for their Majesties King George V and Queen Mary. The bonfire, built mostly of old pit-tubs and planking, was lit at 10 p.m. by Cllr J.L. Joyce JP, Chairman of Hoyland UDC.

Hoyland Law (or Lowe) takes its name from the Anglo-Saxon word *hlaew*, which simply means hill. It is the highest point in Hoyland, rising to 593ft. Hoyland Law is in fact the highest point from Hoyland to the east coast. This distinctive monument, erected at the very top of Law Hill, was built on the instructions of that most prolific builder of great houses, follies and monuments, Thomas Watson-Wentworth, 1st Marquess of Rockingham.

William Fairbanks, who surveyed Hoyland Township in 1771, referred to the stand as 'The Lodge and Bowling Green'. It was certainly used as a hunting lodge. Tankersley Park had a fine herd of red deer and the Townend family of Upper Hoyland Hall had their own pack of staghounds. The Marquess appointed Richard Townend master of game for 'My Manor of Hoyland', but as Lord Rockingham died on 14 December 1750, the same year the stand on Hoyland's Law Hill was completed, he was unable to enjoy the delights of his new tower for long. The tower subsequently became known as Hoyland Law Stand. Building commenced in 1749, shortly after Lord Rockingham purchased the Skiers Hall estate from Viscount Galway, which included land in Upper Hoyland.

It is possible but not very likely that the stand was built on the site of an earlier hunting lodge or folly, giving rise to rumours – which abound locally – that secret tunnels running to Hoyland Law were used during the civil war. It is certainly an important vantage point and may have proved useful during the Battle of Tankersley Moor in 1644.

In 1924 the Dearne Valley Water Board purchased Hoyland Law Stand and some land surrounding it and a reservoir was built on the site of the bowling green. When the last tenant left, the stand was allowed to deteriorate and as the Water Board did not require the monument itself it was eventually sold to Hoyland UDC, which nurtured hopes of restoring the stand and opening it to the public. Unfortunately, that did not happen.

(Sandra Hague Collection)

THIS PRESENT-DAY view of Hoyland Stand shows how much the monument has deteriorated. In recent years Hoyland Lowe Stand Trust was formed with the intention of restoring the entire structure and opening it to the public. In 2010 I was invited to become a patron, along with Sir Michael Parkinson CBE, Granville 'Danny' Clarke FRSA, Dr Sue Kohler BSc dipLD, phd, LittD MBE, and Dickie Bird MBE OBE. A vigorous campaign is underway to raise sufficient funds to carry out a full restoration. The structure is currently protected by high metal railings to prevent unauthorised access and vandalism.

WOMBWELL ROAD, PLATTS COMMON

PLATTS COMMON DID not exist as a village until after the Hoyland Enclosure Acts of the 1790s. It lies between Hoyland and Blacker Hill, and at the time this photograph was taken was served by four public houses and a Working Mens' Club. Sadly, it has never been one of the area's more desirable locations to live, yet within a few yards of its boundary is some spectacular scenery.
(Masheder Family Collection)

TODAY PLATTS COMMON has much diminished, at least from the point of view of its amenities. A light industrial estate occupies the site of two former collieries and three of the four pubs have been demolished, the most recent casualty being the Fighting Cocks. The Pheasant disappeared over a decade ago, and the Union Inn in the 1960s. Only the Royal Oak remains. Several shops and the post office have long since gone. On the right, where there was a gap in the old image, Platts Common's most recent public house stands. Named Sammies, it was fashioned out of the premises once occupied by the now defunct Platts Common Working Men's Club. Recently a planning application has been made to replace Sammies with housing. Apart from a fish and chip shop, Platts Common has little else to recommend it.

UPPER HOYLAND

A 1960s PANORAMIC view of Upper Hoyland and the surrounding countryside. The hamlet of Upper Hoyland (or Over Hoyland, as it is referred to in many early accounts) is inextricably linked with the Townend family, at one time the second largest landowners in the Hoyland township. The largest local property owners had an enormous estate attached to Wentworth Woodhouse, who owned a considerable portion of Hoyland and most of the land in the immediate area surrounding it. The heads of the Townend family were resident at Upper Hoyland Hall, seen in the centre of the photograph. Above the trees to the left can be seen the Perpendicular spire of St Mary's church, Worsborough. On the hillside to the right is Worsborough Bridge and Worsborough Dale. Two thirds along the skyline from the left, the Italianate observation tower in Barnsley's Locke Park is just visible.
(Ivy Conway Collection)

IN THE FORTY years and more that have intervened between the taking of the two images of Upper Hoyland, this once highly desirable, historically important hamlet has been transformed

into a mere shadow of its former self. A proliferation of inappropriate modern housing has been built in both the heart of this small settlement and close to it, some of which can be seen here. The architectural integrity of Upper Hoyland Hall has been radically diminished by these ill-conceived additions to the hamlet. Just out of view to the right, an enormous aircraft hangar-like structure has been built, with no particular purpose in mind other than that one day it might be let. It stands empty, in its enormity, unwanted and unloved. The building of this monstrosity, for rarely could there be a more appropriate use for this word, has caused considerable ill-feeling.

ELSECAR SEEN FROM DISTILLERY SIDE

A LATE NINETEENTH-CENTURY or early twentieth-century view of Elsecar from Distillery Side. The village takes its name from a Saxon lord who owned land in the area. Within the village are the area known as Cobcar, St Helens and Stubbin. Elsecar existed only as scattered farms and cottages until the aristocratic owners of Wentworth Woodhouse began to seriously exploit the area's mineral resources during the eighteenth century, and the creation of a village proper began. In the middle left foreground is the group of ten elegant late eighteenth-century sandstone cottages built by the famous architect John Carr. After the railway came to the village in 1850, these were named Station Row, and the Elsecar goods station, situated across the road from the row of cottages, became established. It is clear from the image that the churchyard extension (opened in 1908) has not yet been created and the construction of the Edwardian

houses in Church Street not yet commenced. The open fields in the centre of the image would be heavily filled in by housing between the two world wars and further building took place in Church Street itself during the 1960s, utilising the last large area of open ground (where I used to go sledging as a boy), when bungalows were built opposite the Wesleyan Reform church. Beacon View was created and Wood View extended at this time. *(Chris Sharp of Old Barnsley)*

SINCE THE CLOSURE of the last remaining coal mines in the area and of mining support facilities locally, a considerable amount of rail track and sidings were removed. Nature, aided by man, has been quick to provide a lush palate of trees and vegetation, greatly enhancing the already much improved air-quality that has existed in the village since the 1980s when heavy industry ceased to be a feature of Elsecar life.

ELSECAR RAILWAY STATION

ELSECAR RAILWAY STATION, *c.* 1910.
The facility was variously known as Elsecar
Station and Elsecar and Hoyland station. It
was opened by the Midland Railway on 1 July
1897. They built shelters on each platform,
with a first-class and a general waiting room.
There were also lavatories for each sex on both
platforms. A goods yard was located on the
right, out of view, with its own sidings. A large
water tank, seen on the left behind the waiting
room roof, was utilised extensively during
the age of steam, and near the bridge on the
left-hand side of the tracks can be seen a water
crane. The gable of the booking office can

be seen on the right. Elsecar was a very well-kept station and won many competitions over the years. Flowers were planted on the two embankments and the platforms were kept in good order. *(Frank Kelly Collection)*

SINCE THE WITHDRAWAL of station staff in the 1960s, Elsecar station has been kept in reasonable order. The goods yards and sidings have long since disappeared. The old waiting rooms were partially demolished and adapted to form new waiting rooms in the 1970s and were completely pulled down and replaced a decade or so later by blue-painted metal structures. At one time these came complete with convenient coin-slot telephones (and later card phones), but unfortunately these were withdrawn due to constant vandalism. The present stainless-steel waiting rooms are fairly recent additions. In the age of the cell phone, on-site public telephones are no longer considered necessary. Some strategically placed public conveniences, however, would not go amiss.

NEWCOMEN-TYPE BEAM ENGINE AND DISTILLERY SIDE

ELSECAR'S CELEBRATED NEWCOMEN-TYPE beam engine in operation, *c.* 1900. The beam engine, situated in the area of Elsecar known as Distillery Side, and named after the coal tar distillery, which operated there from 1814-18, was constructed in 1795 on an adjacent site to Earl Fitzwilliam's Elsecar New Colliery, sunk in the same year. This beam engine is the only engine of its type in the world which remains on its original site. Considered Elsecar's major asset, it is without doubt the most important surviving artefact of South Yorkshire's early industrial expansion. In 1927 Henry Ford paid a secret visit to Elsecar, during a tour which took in several industrial areas throughout this country. His intention was to take exhibits back to the Ford Museum in Detroit. He expressed a strong interest in the engine at Elsecar.

However, someone politely pointed out to Mr Ford that the Elsecar engine was not for sale at any price. The spire of Holy Trinity church is visible above the left-hand side of the engine-house roof. *(Courtesy of Carl Swift)*

TODAY THE NEWCOMEN-TYPE beam engine can only be visited from the perimeter fence. In July 2010 it was put on the Heritage at Risk Register. The failure to capitalise on such an important asset has been a major bone of contention locally for many years. In March 2012 it was announced that a £425,000 Heritage Lottery grant has been awarded to enable a complete restoration to take place. Work will take two years to complete and will involve repairing the engine, shaft and engine house, restoring the Newcomen-type beam engine to working order. This bodes very well for the future of this wonderful early industrial survival and for the adjacent Elsecar Heritage Centre.

ELSECAR WORKSHOPS AND EARL FITZWILLIAM'S PRIVATE RAILWAY STATION

IN 1849, WHEN the 5th Earl Fitzwilliam gave up his interest in Elsecar Ironworks, John Hartop – son of Henry Hartop, who had assumed control of Elsecar Ironworks after his father's departure in 1843 – advised his Lordship that he ought to retain the foundry plant and set up a 'Central Establishment', an engineering workshop to do everything 'new as regards iron and woodwork and the greater proportion of the repairs required for coal and iron mines, and all Machinery, Iron and Heavy Wood work on the whole estate particularly Steam Engines, which should have periodical inspection in order that all needful repairs may be done in due time...'

Work was soon underway to build the complex, part of which is seen here, situated on a site adjacent to the ironworks between there and the Newcomen-type beam engine and Elsecar New Colliery. It was built between 1850 and 1860. John Hartop was appointed manager there. Elsecar Central Workshops became known locally as the New Yard. The car pictured here, carrying their Majesties King George V and Queen Mary, leaves Elsecar Central Workshops, 9 July 1912. The King and Queen were staying at Wentworth Woodhouse during their visit to Yorkshire as guests of Lord and Lady Fitzwilliam. A group of onlookers stand outside the private railway station, built for the 6th Earl Fitzwilliam in 1870. *(Sandra Hague Collection)*

FOLLOWING THE CLOSURE of all the local coal mines during the 1980s, Elsecar Central

Workshops, which had come under the control of the National Coal Board in 1947, closed down. In 1986 the Department of the Environment listed most of the buildings as being of special architectural or historic importance, and in 1988 Barnsley Metropolitan Borough Council purchased the site and began a restoration programme. On Friday, 25 March 1994, following completion of a £1 million restoration of the Power House building, Elsecar Heritage Centre was officially opened by Her Majesty the Queen. As yet the full potential of this historic site and tourist attraction has not been realised and there are mixed feelings locally about its true worth. There is a steam railway, which is very popular, but few other facilities to attract visitors on the scale of those visiting Beamish, or indeed the Black Country Museum. With a little more gumption, Elsecar could easily match, if not outdo, these other attractions.

EARL FITZWILLIAM'S SIMON WOOD COLLIERY

THE FIRST OF the twin pit shafts of Earl Fitzwilliam's Simon Wood Colliery was being sunk when the Barnsley seam was reached at a depth of 93.5yds on 1 September 1853. Known locally as the Planting Pit, it was also called the Bicycle Pit. The two pit shafts were only a few yards apart. The engine house had a headgear coming out of opposite sides, with a single pulley attached. The two winding ropes were attached to the same drum, which caused the pulleys to revolve in the same direction as each other (hence the nickname the Bicycle Pit). This colliery ceased production on 29 May 1903. The EFW Flour Mill, like Simon Wood Colliery, was also built for the 5th Earl in 1842. It can be seen in the left background opposite Holy Trinity Church, which was likewise built at His Lordship's expense. The flour mill produced stone ground flour, which was highly prized far and wide. I can remember EFW Stone Ground Flour being available in shops at Banbury in Oxfordshire when I was visiting my relations there in the 1970s. This steam-powered mill replaced the last wind-powered mill on the Wentworth Estate. The estate sold the mill on 10 December 1962 to Elsecar Stone Ground Flour Mills Limited, a subsidiary of Allied Mills Limited. Behind the colliery chimney can be seen Reform Row. *(George Hardy Collection)*

AT THE SITE of Simon Wood Colliery, spring 2012. The colliery was built right next to the Elsecar Branch of the Dearne and Dove Canal, seen here, close to the canal basin, as was the flour mill, although by that time coal was generally transported by rail along the adjacent track to the colliery forming the Elsecar branch of the South Yorkshire Railway, which opened in 1850. Today there are considerable numbers of trees and thick vegetation in the vicinity, making an exact comparison of then and now images impossible. The spire of Holy Trinity church can be seen, as can the former EFW Flour Mill, now occupied by Kanza Craft, who specialise in high-quality stained glass products.

The canal, seen here in a semi-neglected state, was authorised by Act of Parliament in 1793. Harley Dike was dammed to create Elsecar Reservoir which feeds the canal at Elsecar Basin, and construction of the canal began in January 1795. The canal was used for the transportation of coal, flour, iron and steel products and other locally produced goods (including, for a short period from 1814, lamp black, tar and varnish produced at a works in the area now known as Distillery Side, which was situated near Elsecar Basin, adjacent to the Newcomen-type beam engine). Some restoration work, instigated by a local group, took place on this stretch of the canal more than a decade ago and included the installation of new lock gates. Sadly, after this group disbanded, the canal has been largely neglected.

HOWSE'S CORNER, ELSECAR

HOWSE'S CORNER FROM Forge Lane, Elsecar, *c.* 1895. The name has been used from since about that time after William and Martha Howse, my great-grandparents, opened a confectionary, grocery and general store here. Howse's shop, in the left foreground, is at No. 1 Wentworth Road. Wath Road goes off to the right and Fitzwilliam Street is straight ahead. Elsecar Market Hall, built by the 6th Earl Fitzwilliam and opened on Christmas Eve 1870, can be seen in the right-hand foreground, surrounded by a fence of stone posts and iron railings. The iron bollards placed on the street corners were to prevent carriage wheels mounting the pavement as the coachmen took the corners. William Howse gradually expanded his business interests, and in addition to

the shop he also dealt in insurance. William and Martha had twelve children, eleven of whom survived into adulthood. Two of their daughters eventually took over the running of the business. The younger daughter, Kate, was a popular local figure. She ran a mobile grocery and greengrocery business, visiting the surrounding villages by horse and cart. *(Ann Howse Collection)*

KATE AND SARAH Ann Howse continued running the family business well into the 1960s and into their old age, but following their deaths the property standing at Howse's Corner was demolished. Of the four bollards placed at each corner of the irregular crossroads, only one remains today: it once protected the corner of the New Yard, now Elsecar Heritage Centre. Elsecar Market Hall, renamed Milton Hall in honour of the 7th Earl Fitzwilliam's son and heir, Viscount Milton, today serves as a community centre and is hired out for exhibitions, weddings and other functions.

FITZWILLIAM STREET, ELSECAR

FITZWILLIAM STREET, LOOKING towards Howse's Corner, *c.* 1925. The New Yard can be seen facing the end of the street. On the left is the Miners' Lodging House built by the 5th Earl Fitzwilliam in 1850 to accommodate young, single miners. This was not a successful idea, the miners preferring to live elsewhere. For a short time it was used as a social club and was jocularly known as the 'Bun and Milk Club' as it didn't serve alcohol. That closed in 1854. A boys' club, subsidised by the 6th Earl Fitzwilliam and known as the Low Club, occupied it from 1865. From 1902 the village 'bobby' lived in part of it, at the opposite end of the building to the steward of the boys' club. The middle section became a club for the colliery workshops, but after the Fitzwilliam

mining enterprises were nationalised in 1947, much of the building stood empty. Messrs J. Priestman and Co. Ltd, a burling and weaving company, took over for a few years before Swift's, a local joinery business, traded from there until 1973. The building became severely dilapidated and there was a threat of demolition. The Miners' Lodging House was given Grade ll listed building status on 23 April 1974.
(*Margaret Gaddass Collection*)

FORTUNATELY, A JOINT effort by North Cheshire Housing Association and Barnsley MBC, assisted by a grant from the Department of the Environment, resulted in conversion into fourteen flats. The newly named Fitzwilliam Lodge was officially opened by the Mayor of Barnsley, Cllr John Wake, in 1982. More recently, this fine building has undergone further refurbishment and reconstruction of some of the interior rooms and layout, creating eight apartments. Locals still refer to the building as the 'Bun and Milk Club'. Old habits die hard in Elsecar and Hoyland!

FITZWILLIAM STREET, ELSECAR, CONTINUED

FITZWILLIAM STREET, LOOKING towards the Butchers Arms, in the early twentieth century, showing the splendid properties on the left, which had been built by the Fitzwilliams during the previous century, and some bemused local characters, intent on watching the photographer at work. The Butchers Arms can be seen immediately to the left at the bottom of the street, facing the Miners' Lodging House (which was around the left corner, out of sight). The Fitzwilliam family, notably the 4th, 5th and 6th Earls Fitzwilliam, was responsible for the development of Elsecar

as a village from what was still, towards the end of the eighteenth century, just a few scattered farms and cottages.

The 4th Earl engaged the fashionable and accomplished architect John Carr (1723-1807), often referred to as Carr of York, to produce designs for cottages to house his colliers. Carr submitted designs for six types. Those which were built include what later became known as Station Row, in Wath Road, and four cottages (two semi-detached between two detached), and an eighteenth-century country house (lodge-like in appearance) at Skiers Hall. The cottages seen here are later than Carr's work.
(Chris Sharp of Old Barnsley)

SADLY, SOME OF the Fitzwilliam properties had to be demolished during the 1980s. The lost cottages were deemed to be beyond repair because of severe mining subsidence. The cottages built by the Fitzwilliams that remain are a great asset to Elsecar's appearance. With a little thought, the mistakes of the past could be remedied. It would not be too difficult to rebuild the lost properties in the same style using complementary materials. The Butchers Arms, long since closed, now serves as private residences.

HILL STREET, ELSECAR

HILL STREET (formerly Stubbin), seen from Fitzwilliam Street, *c.* 1900. Church Street goes off to the right, and Foundry Street to the left. During the period of industrial expansion that took place locally during the mid-eighteenth century and for 100 years or so following, the village of Elsecar grew. Many of the houses built laterally on the hillside rising from Church Street to the top of Stubbin, such as Darwins Yard, Evans Terrace, Wards Row, and Back Stubbin, were demolished in the two decades after the Second World War. Some of the buildings below the Fitzwilliam Arms fronting Hill Street remained until the early 1970s, including the Barley Corn, part of which was

latterly occupied by Frank's barber shop, and the Co-op butcher's, which had been relocated to larger premises in Hill Street from Church Street, which also occupied a former public house. At the time when this photograph was taken, this part of Elsecar had no fewer than five public houses – as well as more than half a dozen shops between Church Street and Elsecar railway station, if one includes the Crown Inn. Beer houses, operating from various private residences, were also to be found in the vicinity.

A CONTEMPORARY VIEW of Hill Street. Today there are no shops to be found between Church Street and the railway station, and of the public houses only the Crown Inn and Fitzwilliam Arms remain – although the Royal Oak, once popularly known as Tommy Upsteps after a former landlord (and because one had to climb several iron balustraded steps in order to enter the premises), has survived as a private residence.

NORTH SIDE OF HILL STREET, ELSECAR

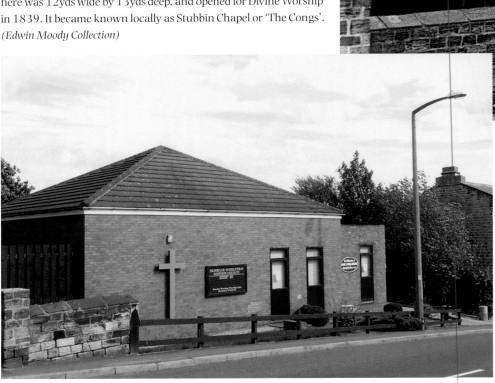

HILL STREET, EARLY twentieth century. An excellent view of the Manse and Elsecar Congregational church. Parkins Yard and the Royal Oak (popularly known as 'Tommy Upsteps') can be seen on the right. Congregational churches are Protestant Christian churches, practicing the belief of Congregationalist church governance, in which each church independently and autonomously runs its own affairs, a movement which has its origins in a theory of union published by the theologian Robert Browne in 1592. Built to the designs of York-based architect James Pigott Pritchett (1789-1868), who was briefed to design a plain Gothic building to serve as a chapel and school, the building seen here was 12yds wide by 13yds deep, and opened for Divine Worship in 1839. It became known locally as Stubbin Chapel or 'The Congs'. *(Edwin Moody Collection)*

ON 4 JANUARY 1966, Stubbin Chapel became part of the Congregational church in England and Wales, and in 1972 the structure of Congregationalism changed with the joining together of Congregationalists and Presbyterians. The new title of 'United Reform church' was then adopted. By 1975 the church fabric was causing concern due to damage caused by severe mining subsidence, and it became necessary for the NCB (National Coal Board) to shore up the building. Within days of this happening the building became too dangerous to enter and demolition became the only option. In 1976 the congregation voted overwhelmingly to rebuild the church on the same site. Compensation was agreed with the NCB and John Brunton & Partners, architects and surveyors, of Leeds, designed the new building and the local building firm R. Vickers & Co., Hoyland, carried out the construction. Elsecar United Reform church's dwindling congregation resulted in the final service being held on 29 February 2004, and a 164-link with Congregationalism in Elsecar came to an end. Later that same year Elsecar Wesleyan Reform church moved from their original premises in Church Street and relocated in the building seen here in Hill Street.

ELECTRA PALACE, ELSECAR

THE ELECTRA PALACE opened in Elsecar in 1914 at the top of Stubbin. It had stalls seating only, with double seats towards the rear favoured by courting couples. This cinema changed its name in the 1930s to the Futurist, a name which it kept until its closure as a cinema in 1986.
(George Hardy Collection)

THE BUILDING WAS refurbished in the late 1980s and briefly traded as a pool hall and video-games establishment. This enterprise, however, was short-lived and the building stood empty for several years until it was taken over by a private individual who uses it to house his collection of vintage vehicles. To the left of the cinema building at No. 60 Hill Street is a small shop that, for many years, was Cutts' butchers. At the time of writing the little shop was occupied by Jacqui's Sweet Box, alas a short-lived enterprise trading for just a few months. The business closed during the production of this book. Beyond the old cinema, in what for many years was Wainwright's chemists, is Electra Hair & Beauty Salon and beyond, in premises once occupied by the King Street branch of the Co-operative grocery, is Assura Pharmacy.

CHURCH STREET, ELSECAR

CHURCH STREET, 1890s. On the right, the tall roof of the first large gable is that of the butcher's shop, grocery store and manager's house of the Elsecar branch of the Barnsley British Co-operative Society. The second gable belongs to the Wesleyan Reform Chapel, built in 1859. The new brick-built boys' section of Elsecar Church of England School, built thanks to the benevolence of the 6th Earl Fitzwilliam, masks the older mixed school, which was built in dressed sandstone in 1852, as a larger replacement for a school built by the 5th Earl Fitzwilliam in 1836 on Distillery Side. Holy Trinity

church can be seen beyond. A long empty tract of land stretches all the way from the end of the terrace on the left as far as the new school building. Holy Trinity church, built in Early English style at his own expense by the 5th Earl Fitzwilliam, at a cost of £2,500, opened for worship on Whit Monday, 6 June 1843.
(Chris Thawley Collection)

CHURCH STREET IN the present day is much altered. Early twentieth century housing sprang up between the Church of England School and a new road joining Church Street to Cobcar Lane known as Zetland Road, named in honour of the 7th Earl Fitzwilliam's father-in-law, the Marquess of Zetland. Other dwellings sprang up later in the twentieth century, filling Church Street's remaining green-field sites, and some of the older houses were replaced by the modern dwellings seen here.

WATH ROAD, ELSECAR

WATH ROAD, SEEN here in the early twentieth century. The wall in the left foreground encloses the churchyard of Holy Trinity church. The Ship Inn forms part of the terrace built for the 4th Earl Fitzwilliam in around 1785-90, and known as Meadow Row.
(Keith Robinson Collection)

THE EIGHTEENTH-CENTURY Ship Inn was demolished between the two world wars and replaced by the present set-back, brick-built Ship Inn. The remaining cottages in Meadow Row form one of, if not the oldest, group of cottages to survive in the village. During the production of this book the Ship Inn closed. The building has been sold, and is in the process of being converted into a five-bedroom house.

SKIERS HALL

THE SKIERS FAMILY takes its name from the hamlet within Hoyland's boundaries. Skiers Hall, seen here during the 1920s, long after many of its finer features had been degentrified and this once grand house converted into cottages, dated from the fourteenth century.

The Skiers Hall Estate remained in the Skiers family during the medieval period and various members appear on documents connected with land throughout the area. One family member who hailed from the hall, Nicholas Skiers (spelled Skeres in some contemporary accounts), was in the employ of Sir Francis Walsingham, Elizabeth I's spymaster. Skiers had been involved in the uncovering of 'The Babbington Plot', a scheme to assassinate the queen and replace her with the imprisoned Roman Catholic Mary Queen of Scots. On 31 May 1593, he was at Deptford in the company of the renowned poet and dramatist Christopher Marlowe and three other men, including Ingram Frizer (all connected to Walsingham), when Marlowe was stabbed through the eye by a dagger wielded by Frizzer, dying instantly. There has been much speculation concerning these events through the centuries.

This postcard view was published as one of a large series of South Yorkshire views, by Hoyland confectioner and newsagent Lichie Walker, with photography by Roy Colville. (*Walker's Newsagents Collection*)

UNFORTUNATELY, SKIERS HALL itself was demolished in 1951. This image shows the site of Skiers Hall today. The hamlet of Skiers Hall comprises Skiers Hall Farm and three adjacent cottages, and across a dirt track from the farmyard buildings just four other dwellings, these being the eighteenth-century lodge-like cottages built to the designs of one of England's greatest architects, John Carr, who carried out major projects on the extensive Wentworth Estate, firstly for Charles Watson-Wentworth, 2nd Marquess of Rockingham, and afterwards for his nephew and heir, William, 4th Earl Fitzwilliam, whose lands the Skiers Hall Estate had become part of.

RAINBOROUGH
GRANGE

A 1930s VIEW of Rainborough Grange, in Brampton Bierlow, close to its border with Hoyland township. Substantial buildings existed here for over 900 years, from before the time when the monks of Monk Bretton Priory (founded in 1153) established a grange at Rainborough on land given by Alan Fitzswain. The first Rainborough Grange was built at the head of a field known as the Starbank, situated close to Rainborough Park, from stone quarried on its own estate, which involved adapting a substantial building that predated the Domesday Survey of 1086. The Rainborough Grange that replaced it, seen here, probably dates from the sixteenth or early seventeenth century and was built further down the hill, a short distance from the quarry that provided the stone for all the buildings on the estate. Rainborough Grange (a grange is simply a country house with farm buildings attached) can be seen in the middle of the photograph. The quarry, which was situated slightly out of view to the left, had a sheer drop to the deep workings.

After the Dissolution of the Monasteries (1538), Monk Bretton Priory's various estates passed to new owners. The Rainborough Grange Estate eventually came under the ownership of the Wentworth family of Wentworth Woodhouse. Open-cast mining, which took place nearby in 1943, mostly destroyed the natural

springs, causing drainage problems on the Rainborough Grange Estate, and making the land difficult to farm. Rainborough Grange and part of its estate were sold to the National Coal Board after fears were raised of subsidence, in order that the tip could be extended and its extremities secured. The entire site seen in his image was covered over by colliery waste in 1967, creating an ugly purple and grey slag heap.
(Courtesy of George W. Cooke and Mrs Kathleen M. Robinson)

TODAY THE FORMER tip pit is clad in a luscious green blanket, and Rainborough Grange, with all its history, lies beneath. No longer slag heap-like in appearance, this mound has taken on the contours similar to many of the natural features that abound in the neighbouring countryside. Hoober Stand can be seen at the top of Hoober Hill in the extreme left background. Following the closure of collieries throughout the area during the 1980s, the site is once again in the ownership of the Fitzwilliam (Wentworth) Estates, as these vast estates are presently known.

HARLEY

OCCUPATION ROAD, HARLEY, seen here in the early twentieth-century. Harley is a small village (and should probably be more correctly termed a hamlet) sandwiched between Tankersley Park and the larger country estate village of Wentworth, with one public house, the Horseshoe, situated at the corner of Occupation Road, at the junction of Harley Road. Harley lies within the civil parish of Wentworth. The Hauslin family lived in Harley for nearly four centuries and were one-time residents of Harley Hall. Situated on Dyke Hill, it was recorded in 1587 as Harley Hall, the Grange of Hoyland, one of the possessions of Thomas Wentworth of Wentworth Woodhouse.
(Chris Sharp of Old Barnsley)

A CENTURY LATER, the buildings in Occupation Road are externally substantially unaltered. However, the integrity of these mostly Victorian buildings, and Harley's earlier buildings, has been severely compromised by a modern development. The contrast between Harley and neighbouring Wentworth remains the object of puzzlement to the many sightseers, walkers and tourists visiting the area. However, the planning *faux pas* encountered in Harley's expansion is not untypical of many small towns and villages in this part of Yorkshire.

BLACKER HILL

AN EARLY TWENTIETH-CENTURY view of Wentworth Road, Blacker Hill. Blacker Hill post office is in the left foreground. The Blacksmith's Arms is next to it, and a little further down the street is the Travellers'. Across the road is Blacker Hill Working Men's Club. The Mission Hall and Blacker Hill Chapel are in the left distance. The area known as Blacker – and the hill that rises above it, from which the village takes its name, Blacker Hill – lies beyond Platts Common, between there and Dovecliffe and the village of Worsborough, adjacent to Wombwell Wood. A settlement of sorts has existed in the vicinity for centuries – indeed, in 2003 archaeologists from York discovered evidence of an Iron Age settlement in the ancient woodland bordering Blacker Hill, believed to be over 5,000 years old, and Roman coins dating from AD 180 to AD 350 were discovered in nearby Dovecliffe quarry. A few of the properties in the village itself date from the eighteenth

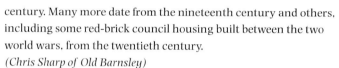

century. Many more date from the nineteenth century and others, including some red-brick council housing built between the two world wars, from the twentieth century.
(Chris Sharp of Old Barnsley)

THE HEAVY INDUSTRIES which proliferated around Blacker Hill, including coal mines and a large coking plant, have not been a feature of the village for over two decades. Since their demise the air around the village has become infinitely sweeter, and the once almost permanently smoky atmosphere, which seemed to imbue the village with an unpleasantly grey hue, has also disappeared. Sadly, many of the amenities the village once possessed have also gone. The Blacksmith's Arms and the Travellers' are now private residences. The Working Men's Club has also disappeared, as has the Co-operative grocery store, the village school, post office, and all the village's other shops. One public house remains: the Royal Albert. The chapel which replaced the one seen in the older image, faced with a severely depleted congregation, closed its doors in 2011. Despite these losses, Blacker Hill continues to develop and is gradually evolving into an attractive village, with some highly motivated residents ensuring the tremendous community spirit, a feature of the village for generations, remains at the forefront.

WENTWORTH

MAIN STREET, WENTWORTH, *c*.1900. Four Saxon lords had shares
in the 'Winterworth' estate, Wentworth's name in the Domesday
Survey of 1086. The name Wentworth has two interpretations. The
first is a pleasant abode, 'went' signifying fair or white and 'worth'
a dwelling place; the other is a high but cultivated spot, where the
cold was severe but the land productive. From at least as early as
the thirteenth century the village has been inextricably linked with
Wentworth Woodhouse, the stately home that lies within Wentworth
Park, which was, until 1979, occupied by members of the
Wentworth family and their descendants, the Watson-Wentworths
and the Wentworth-Fitzwilliams. The village and its satellite hamlets
evolved to suit the changing requirements of the great house and
estate which its inhabitants served. The Wentworths and their
descendants also played a considerable part in the development of
Hoyland and many of the surrounding villages. Main Street was
once known as 'The Town Street'. In the left foreground is part of
the complex of buildings belonging to the George and Dragon Hotel,

and on the right is Pole's shop, which was the village's principal shop for over 100 years, until the
Barnsley British Co-operative Society took over the premises in 1916
(Sandra Hague Collection)

ALTHOUGH WENTWORTH WOODHOUSE, described in *Country Life* in February 2010 as
probably the largest private house in the world and one of the largest classical buildings of any
type, is now in the ownership of the Newbold family, the vast Fitzwilliam (Wentworth) Estates
remains in control of the Wentworth family's descendants: the heirs of the 8th and 10th Earls
Fitzwilliam. The estate covers huge tracts of land around Wentworth and the Hoyland area.
Main Street was tarmacadamised in 1914. The George and Dragon – now minus the hotel epithet
it once adopted – is still a major village feature. The Co-op grocery store traded in Pole's former
premises until February 1974. These premises are currently occupied by a retail business known
as The Village Shop. Across the road, in a building that forms part of the George and Dragon
complex of buildings that for many years was occupied by the village's only butcher, is now a
wine merchant's.

JUMP HALL FARM
AND LILAC CRESCENT

JUMP HALL FARM, seen here in the early twentieth century. Jump Hole Farm (which later became Jump Hall Farm) is mentioned in the Wentworth Manor Court Rolls of 1576. Jumble Hole, which in old English dialect meant a rough, bushy, uncultivated hollow, has been cited as the origin of the name Jump (among other, less likely theories). There was a lintel with the

date 1510 emblazoned across it in an older part of the house. The farm was situated just within Hoyland township. In 1605 Richard Townend of Blacker bequeathed to Robert Swinden two fields lying in the enclosed area known as High Fields, in the township of Wombwell; at that time they were being used by John Hill, who lived at Jump or Jump Hole Farm. In 1723 another John Hill sold to his son Thomas Jump Farm. In 1749, Thomas Hill and Sir William Wentworth, Bt, of Bretton Hall, signed an indenture concerning Jump Farm. A gravestone in Wentworth churchyard reads: 'Thomas Hill of Jump, Gent, died 6 November 1755'.

In 1771 William Shaw owned Jump Farm, and in 1842, when William Vizard wanted to make a railway incline from Hoyland Silkstone Colliery to Elsecar Canal basin, he bought land belonging to Jump Farm from another William Shaw, of Great Houghton. The last tenant of Jump Hall Farm was Bernard Hazelwood, who rented it from the trustees of the late Richard Wadsworth, one-time landlord of the Rockingham Arms, Wentworth. Jump Hall Farm was taken off the rating list in 1954 and was demolished soon afterwards. *(Keith Hopkinson collection)*

THE SITE OF Jump Hall Farm today. Behind the single-storey building, originally built as a Co-operative grocery store and currently occupied by a take-away outlet, hairdresser's and Premier corner shop, is Lilac Crescent.

CHURCH STREET, JUMP

AN EARLY TWENTIETH-CENTURY view of Church Street,
Jump. When asked, 'Where do you come from?', many 'Jumpers'
have been faced with shrieks of laughter when they have replied
'Jump'. This laughter stems from surprise at this most unusual
of place names. Astonished travellers, driving along the B6096,
are confronted by the road sign declaring, 'Jump, 1 mile'. There
are many theories concerning the origins of the name, but the
evidence points to all these theories stemming from nearby
Jump Hall Farm. Before 1800 the village of Jump did not exist. It
was not until after 1830 that the village began to take shape.

It was coal mining that was ultimately responsible for
the foundation of the village itself. Mining had been taking
place in Jump Valley since the middle of the eighteenth
century, during the time of the 1st and 2nd Marquesses of
Rockingham. There were drifts into the valley sides or shallow
mines, which worked coal that outcropped close to the surface.
The 2nd Lord Rockingham's nephew and heir, William, 4th
Earl Fitzwilliam, opened his Jump Colliery, which worked the
Barnsley bed seam, in 1816. The expansion of that mine in
the years that followed, and the opening of other mines in the
vicinity, gradually led to the development of more housing in
the area. From about 1850, the Dawes family, who leased both

Elsecar and Milton Ironworks from Lord Fitzwilliam, were responsible for the rapid development of housing in Jump. The house with its gable end on Church Street forms part of the terraces that formed Milton Square (known locally as 'Turkey', many village streets being nicknamed after skirmishes during the Crimean War of 1854-6), whose last occupant was the Dewsnapp family. *(Chris Sharp of Old Barnsley)*

TODAY THE CAR park of Jump Children & Adult Learning Centre occupies the site of the former post office. Beyond, houses that once comprised part of 'Turkey' is Leanne's unisex hair design salon, Cookson's fish and chip shop and Turner's butchers. Percy Turner opened his shop in Church Street in 1937 and today it is run by Percy's sons Percy Junior and Barry. Turner's are famous throughout South Yorkshire for their pork pies, which can be found on sale at shops and market stalls scattered across a wide area. During the lead up to the festive season it is not unusual to see a long queue of customers outside this unassuming butcher's shop from as early as five o'clock in the morning. The white painted gable in the right distance belongs to the Coach & Horses, one of three survivors of Jump's five original public houses. There were also several private residences selling beer. Jump also has a large Working Mens' Club, situated nearby in Wentworth Road.

THE GREEN, HEMINGFIELD

AN EARLY TWENTIETH-CENTURY view of The Green, Hemingfield. A solitary schoolboy poses on the unmetalled road for the photographer. Straddling the hillside above Elsecar and Brampton Bierlow, and lying outside Hoyland's border – within Wombwell township, and between Jump and Wombwell – this once gloomy little village was at that time surrounded by coal mines and heavy industry. There was Hemingfield Colliery itself, situated in the valley below, and nearby, Earl Fitzwilliam's Elsecar Main Colliery, Wombwell Main, Cortonwood Colliery, and on the outskirts of the village, Wombwell Foundry.
(Chris Sharp of Old Barnsley)

MANY OF THE buildings seen in the older image remain. The Albion public house, seen in the left foreground, is a popular survivor, much frequented by locals. Considerable development took place throughout the village during the twentieth century. Several large detached houses have been built at various points around the village periphery. Recently, Hemingfield has suffered greatly and much of its attractiveness is considered by some severely diminished by the installation of unsightly solar panels on the pitched roofs on several of its larger properties.

BIRDWELL

BIRDWELL COMMON, at the junction of The Walk with Sheffield Road, in the early twentieth century. The first known mention of the village of Birdwell was in 1642, during the civil war. It is not known exactly from where the name derives, but a local belief holds that some servants from nearby Tankersley Hall found a well of clear water. When they saw some birds drinking from it they decided the water must be pure and fit to drink, and began using the well themselves for drinking water, naming it 'bird well'. The name may also have its origins in the Anglo-Saxon *Brydd-Wella*, which means bird well. The site of this ancient well is today covered by the M1

Motorway. Junction 36 of the motorway is at Birdwell and lies less than a quarter of a mile from where this image was taken.
(Chris Sharp of Old Barnsley)

SHEFFIELD ROAD IS the main thoroughfare in Birdwell. Ninety-five per cent of travellers passing through the village are only likely to see this part of it, which is – for the most part – Birdwell's most unimpressive feature. It is in the side streets that Birdwell's more attractive, historic and interesting features are to be found. Sheffield Road appears substantially the same a century after the old image was taken. Flowers of Distinction occupies the shop in the right foreground. The vast majority of houses have considerable charm.

Other titles published by The History Press

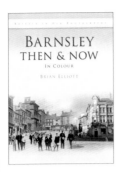

Barnsley Then & Now

BRIAN ELLIOT

Founded on an eighteenth-century industrial heritage of wire, linen, glass and coal, the Barnsley of today is much altered, and some parts are now almost beyond recognition. Placing amazing archive images alongside beautiful modern photography and detailed captions, Brian Elliott explores what Barnsley has lost but also what it has gained in some of the positive new developments that are contributing to a new Barnsley – now a twenty-first-century market town.

978 0 7524 6402 2

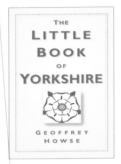

The Little Book of Yorkshire

GEOFFREY HOWSE

A fascinating, fact-packed compendium of the sort of information which no-one will want to be without. The county's most eccentric inhabitants, famous sons and daughters, royal connections and literally hundreds of intriguing facts about Yorkshire's landscape, cities, towns and villages come together to make one handy, pocket-sized treasure trove of trivia. A remarkably engaging little book, this is essential reading for visitors and locals alike.

978 0 7524 5773 4

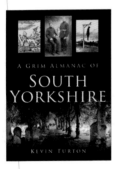

A Grim Almanac of South Yorkshire

KEVIN TURTON

A Grim Almanac of South Yorkshire is a collection of stories from the county's past, some bizarre, some fascinating, some macabre, but all equally absorbing. Revealed here are the dark corners of the county, where witches, body snatchers, highwaymen and murderers, in whatever guise, have stalked. Accompanying this cast of gruesome characters are old superstitions, omens, strange beliefs and long-forgotten remedies for all manner of ailments.

978 0 7524 5678 2

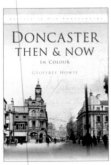

Doncaster Then & Now

GEOFFREY HOWSE

Doncaster thrived during the Georgian period, and continued to grow as a railway town in the nineteenth century. As a consequence, it can boast a rich architectural history, the influence of which can still be seen and appreciated in the fabric of the Doncaster of the modern day. Geoffrey Howse's comparisons between archive images of the Doncaster of decades past and modern photographs of the same scenes today beautifully illustrates the changing face of this historic town, as well as the changes in society, transport and fashions.

978 0 7524 6347 6

Visit our website and discover thousands of other History Press books.

www.thehistorypress.co.uk